HERCULANEUM & SARDANAPALUS

Borgo Press Books by FRANK J. MORLOCK

Castor and Pollux and Other Opera Libretti (Editor)
The Chevalier d'Éon and Other Short Farces (Editor)
Chuzzlewit
Congreve's Comedy of Manners
Crime and Punishment
Cyrano and Molière: Five Plays by or About Molière (Editor)
Falstaff (with Shakespeare, John Dennis, & William Kendrick)
Fathers and Sons
Herculaneum & Sardanapalus: Two Opera Libretti (Editor)
The Idiot
Isle of Slaves and Other Plays (Editor)
Jurgen
Justine
The Londoners & The Green Carnation: Two Plays
Lord Jim
The Madwoman of Beresina and Other Napoleonic Plays (Editor)
Notes from the Underground
Oblomov
Old Creole Days
Outrageous Women: Lady Macbeth and Other Plays (Editor)
Peter and Alexis
The Princess Casamassima
A Raw Youth
Salammbô & Dido: Two Operas (Editor)
The Stendhal Hamlet Scenarios and Other Shakespearean Shorts from the French (Editor)
Two Voltairean Plays: The Triumvirate; and, Comedy at Ferney (Editor)
The Widow's Husband; and, Porthos in Search of an Outfit: Two Dumasian Comedies (Editor)
Zeneida & The Follies of Love & The Cat Who Changed into a Woman: Two Plays (Editor)

HERCULANEUM & SARDANAPALUS

TWO OPERA LIBRETTI

FRANK J. MORLOCK, EDITOR

THE BORGO PRESS
MMXIII

HERCULANEUM & SARDANAPALUS

Copyright © 2012, 2013 by Frank J. Morlock

FIRST EDITION

Published by Wildside Press LLC

www.wildsidebooks.com

DEDICATION

To My Good Friend, Victor Lantang

CONTENTS

HERCULANEUM, by Joseph Méry 9
CAST OF CHARACTERS 11
ACT I, Scene 1 13
ACT II, Scene 2 39
ACT III, Scene 3 55
ACT IV, Scene 4 77
ACT IV, Scene 5 83
SARDANAPALUS, by Henri Becque 97
CAST OF CHARACTERS 99
ACT I, Scene 1 101
ACT II, Scene 2 119
ACT III, Scene 3 139
ACT III, Scene 4 145
ACT III, Scene 5 155
ABOUT THE EDITOR 157

HERCULANEUM
BY JOSEPH MÉRY,
Music by T. Hadot

CAST OF CHARACTERS

Helios

Nicanor

Satan (under the features of Nicanor)

Magnus

Satan

Olympia

Lilia

Court of Olympia

Kings, Satraps. Princes, People, Christians, Slaves, Lictors, Guards, etc.

CHARACERS in the BALLET

Daphnes

Erigone

The Muses, The Graces, Bacchantes, Sylvians, Priests of Bacchus, etc.

ACT I
SCENE 1

Herculaneum, A.D. 79.

An elustrian peristyle of the palace of Olympia. The valeria suspend friezes from heights, sheltering the Queen's gardens against the ardor of the Sun. In the Egyptian quarter, the features of the Sphinx can be made out, neighboring the port where vessels loaded with the Delta's incense dock.

In the back, villas, temples, palaces; consular houses rise in a sort of amphitheater.

CHORUS

Glory, glory to you great queen

Queen of nations and of kings.

The Orient to its sovereign

Speaks today in our voice.

The world is conquered by your charms.

Your beauty is your power.

Cupids are your weapons.

Your goddess is sensuality.

NICANOR

Olympia, my sister! Parthenope is on holiday.

All Italy applauds your beauty.

Your august head is girdled with laurels and myrtle.

You, queen by grace and by majesty,

Rome to your gentle laws submits a vast empire.

Fools say the old world is expiring.

You make the voice of pleasure reborn in it.

CHORUS

Glory to you, great queen.

NICANOR

Vainly vile Christians call down on your fests,

Fire which will devour ancient cities.

Up till now, the lightning has struck only their heads.

Your arms annihilate their detested altars;

They fall—beneath a power greater than their funereal might;

None comes to seize from your hands

This glorious scepter—the only scepter which remains.

Queen of beauty, goddess of pleasure.

CHORUS

Glory, glory to you, great queen!

OLYMPIA

Yes, o my brother, I crossed the seas to come,

To invest myself with a power that I owe to Romans.

Illustrious Proconsul, it is twice dearer to me,

This royal purple, in passing through your hands.

It's you, you that the Euphrates, just like me, sees born,

And that Rome adopts as one of its children.

It's you, dear Nicanor, you who cause to reappear

In the oriental heaven our triumphant stars.

(Enter Satraps, Princes, and Kings, tributaries of Olympia, who prostrate themselves before her.)

NICANOR

To celebrate the days on which my noble sister

Founds this new empire promised by destiny,

Satraps, Princes, and Kings representing the world—

The Queen invites you to the delights of the feast.

CHORUS OF PEOPLE

Blood! Blood!

Do Justice.

Their crime is great.

Quick to torture, execution.

Blood! Blood!

OLYMPIA

What are they doing?

CHORUS

They are sectaries

Of those who defy your laws,

Celebrating odious mysteries.

OLYMPIA

Allow them to come to me.

NICANOR

Beneath their humble clothes I was able to recognize him,

A vassal prince of Rome, and yours,

Born to wear the purple and speak as master,

He prefers to make himself a slave by making himself Christian.

OLYMPIA

Answer me, speak—is this your crime?

Have you scorned my rule?

Is it possible pride can drive you to this degree?

I am just—answer me!

HELIOS

In a profound retreat

I lived, bound by an oath,

And asked nothing of the world,

Save the happiness of being forgotten,

With no other hope to sustain me.

In the aurora at twilight,

I adore a Christian girl.

My only crime is my love.

LILIA

In a profound retreat,

By faith my heart is bound.

And far from the world, I adore

The true god, everywhere forgotten,

With no other hope to sustain me,

In the depth of my humble dwelling.

I intend to be faithful to the Christian faith—until the

last day.

NICANOR

Your god, your faith are extinguished errors;

And bad luck to those who relight them.

All sensuality—those are holy things.

Confess—the only gods that I here name

Or prepare to die!

OLYMPIA

No! Enough of terror.

I am weary of blood. Besides, what do they care

About death? They have faith, this lie from the heart.

Christians always believe heaven is opening its gate

And that death renders them victors over their executioners.

They shall live.

NICANOR

They shall live!

OLYMPIA

It's necessary to tame their soul.

To strike the body is nothing. She will succumb—

(looking at Helios)

As for him, I intend, despite her passion

To be—the god that he adores—before tonight.

Go—leave with my court.

NICANOR

My noble sister orders it.

Let's take places at the feast she is offering us.

OLYMPIA (to Helios and Lilia)

You, stay.

What are the names they call you?

HELIOS

Helios.

LILIA

Lilia.

OLYMPIA

The Queen pardons you.

HELIOS (aside)

How beautiful she is!

OLYMPIA

For you my heart is softened.

Fear nothing—I intend to forget an outrage,

And I know what indulgence is owed to your age.

LILIA

Her pardon shocks me—and I don't know why.

OLYMPIAS

Helios, my glance has fallen on you.

I want to change your fate. For a moment, stay.

(to Lilia)

And you, you may freely leave the palace.

HELIOS (to Lilia)

Till tonight.

Go—I will rejoin you.

LILIA

(low)

Come at the first hour.

HELIOS

Near sacred tombs—under the shining, and luminous Pharos.

Whose shining shines only for us, children of prayer,

I shall find you.

LILIA

I'll wait for you on my knees,

At the foot of the Holy Cross, knees on stone.

HELIOS

Goodbye for a moment.

LILIA

My God, watch over us!

(Lilia leaves)

OLYMPIA

Noble Helios—in your absence,

In vain I sought in my court

A king worthy of my power,

A king worthy of my love.

I've found feigned tenderness;

Truth no longer has altars.

Noble passions are extinguished,

In the hearts of all mortals.

TOGETHER

You remained pure in the house of infamy,

Recognize the rule of our gods!

This palace shall have only two souls.

The world shall have only two voices.

HELIOS

What a brilliant flame

To the sound of her voice,

Lights in my soul

For the first time!

Hell is in my heart—

OLYMPIA

Answer!

HELIOS

I will withdraw.

OLYMPIA

I understand—too much splendor must dazzle your eyes.

Dare to look at me—Hope!

HELIOS

What to say to her?

I seek aid which only comes from heaven.

OLYMPIA

All is submissive to my power;

The universe is at my feet.

You, who owe everything to my clemency,

Fear it may change into wrath.

A power full of mystery

Yields everywhere to my conquering charms.

I am the idol of the earth,

And queen of all hearts.

This is the power which makes me beautiful,

To seduce all and charm all.

One alone would rebel against me,

The only one that I can love!

Brave the anathema of your god, Helios,

Desert his realm.

You can climb to the supreme rock,

And seat yourself by the throne of kings.

HELIOS

Goddess of pleasure, terrible enchantress,

From where does your funereal and magic power

come?

From where do you get this glance that tortures and caresses?

I was strong—before seeing you.

OLYMPIA

Come sit at the feast! Your place is prepared.

We lose nothing of life that gives us time.

Come—in this dwelling consecrated to joy,

Follow the voice that calls you.— Helios, I'm waiting for you.

HELIOS (moving abruptly away from Olympia)

Oh, heaven! What was I going to do?

Ah, my sleeping strength

Awakens. Never to this profane place,

Will I follow the steps of this impious queen.

Never shall I love the enemies of god.

CHORUS

Honor to our queen,

To our sovereign.

OLYMPIA

The joyous guests drink from a full cup

Oriental liqueurs are exhausted at the feast,

In my honor.— Come closer, you must drink to the queen.

Drink to her glorious destiny,

Drink this wine that love gives.

In Autumn,

Each drop, with vermillion tint,

Is a fire that singes us.

An ecstasy,

A smile of sunshine.

Drink this wine! The fecund vine,

Ripened in the cradle of the Sun—

For Venus, daughter of the waves,

The blonde mother of Cupid.

Yes, this wine, celestial counselor.

Tells us all to seize it,

The only remaining truth,

The sweet intoxication of pleasure.

Drinking this wine—one forgets

The sad moments past.

The whole charm which links memory to us is effaced.

Memory is ravished from us.

We are reborn, cup in hand.

To each day of our life, succeeds a more beautiful tomorrow.

(Olympia presents the cup to Helios who hesitates.)

Helios! Obey when the queen orders.

HELIOS

You wish it? Well—give it here!

I drink to the celestial virtue

That comes to my aid from on high.

Yes, strong in the faith that remains in me,

I drink to chaste love—

(Helios drinks. No sooner does he empty the cup than he is seized by a ravishing ecstasy.)

God—what a new world! What a splendid domain!

What Sun dazzles my eyes!

Whose soft voice or hand guides us

Toward the sublime azure of the heavens.

On divine knees my head rested.

The heavens are open for me.

No more terrors! The celestial dawn

Extinguishes the flames of Hell.

CHORUS

The enchanted brew

Gives him happiness.

HELIOS

To you, goddess or queen,

I cede my intoxication.

Goodbye, mad wisdom—

Goodbye, vain lies!

My reason is ravished from me—

And all that I want

Is to spend my life

At your divine knees.

To your power, I surrender myself.

In this air which intoxicates me,

With you I wish to live.

With ambrosia and honey,

Under the hand which binds me—

To never forget you.

Virtue, somber madness!

This earth is heaven.

I want to live forever in the air you breathe.

Goddess of sensuality,

My stars are your eyes, my rays, your smile.

My Sun will be your beauty.

In these flower gardens, ecstasy is embalmed.

The shade is tepid, the lawn is sweet.

Seeing you loved by a mortal,

The angels of heaven are jealous!

(he falls by his knees next to Olympia.)

OLYMPIA

Speak again, Helios, my ear is charmed.

Remain always at my knees!

Yes, speak, speak again! On a beloved lip

The word "love" is so sweet.

CHORUS

This enchanting brew

Gives him happiness.

(Olympia drags Helios toward the fest hall. Enter Magnus. Olympia remains alone.)

OLYMPIA

Who's this stranger?

MAGNUS

He's coming to disturb your feast.

And no one is powerful enough,

To make him bow his head.

Under threat of death,

His voice, echoed by God, will make you bow yours.

God wants to explain to you—in your last moments

The divine book written at Patmos by the Apostle,

The Book of Revelation!

(Suddenly, heaven darkens)

Listen and tremble.

CHORUS

We are listening

And we are trembling.

OLYMPIA

We're listening

And laughing.

MAGNUS

An angel appeared to me and said:

"I will show you the condemnation of

The Whore of Babylon—with whom the kings of

The earth have drunk the wine of debauchery.

And this woman was dressed in purple

And scarlet trimmed in gold

And precious stones—and I saw her

Intoxicated with the blood of Saints and martyrs.

And I saw an angel descend from heaven

Holding in his hands

The key to the abyss,

And having opened It, he unchained the dawn

That the Son of God had enchained.

OLYMPIA, NICANOR, CHORUS

We are listening

And we are laughing.

MAGNUS

This woman in heat to ruin the world,

Olympia—it's you, all soiled

With the blood of Christians, and you, who in a shameless path

Attempt to drag down those God has taken to support.

Queen, and, you, Proconsul, accomplice of her crimes—

Believe and repent!

The time has come! The time has come!

Or to punish you, from the depths of the abyss,

The spirit of evil will emerge today.

OLYMPIA

Open the abyss.

I want to see it.

The God of Crime,

Archangel of Darkness.

(One hears a subterranean noise, like thunder. Vaporous rays arise on the horizon.)

CHORUS

We are listening,

We are trembling.

MAGNUS

Do you hear that? The earth under your feet already scolds.

The sea roars in the distance.

Mountains are seen trembling.

Vesuvius is turning into a burning crater

Ready to swallow all under the fire of demons!

OLYMPIA

We laugh at this prophet

Who comes to charm the feast,

And not to disturb it.

In our days of folly

This Italian buffoon,

Ruins our meals.

Let's forget him

And laugh!

CHORUS

Let's pay attention to the prophet

Who comes to disturb our feast,

And let's not irritate him.

So that Heaven will forget

One day our folly

And not punish us.

Let's listen

And be humble.

MAGNUS

Laugh at this prophet

Who charms your fest.

And don't listen to him

So that, in your folly.

Each of you forgets

Death which follows in his footsteps.

Forget

And laugh.

TOGETHER: OLYMPIA, NICANOR, CHORUS (in counterpoint with MAGNUS [shown below])

Let's forget.

And laugh

At the prophet

Yes, but without him

Today

Our fest

Would extinguish

And cease

Incomplete

Let's forget

And laugh.

MAGNUS

Listen

And tremble

Over your heads

The lighting blazes

In the night

In your fests

The frozen air

Has passed

Over your heads

Listen

And tremble!

(Magnus points to heaven with a threatening gesture.)

CURTAIN

ACT II
SCENE 2

A wild and deserted site in the valley of Ottayano. A tumulus covered with the trunks of columns, ruins, misshapen stones, surmounted by a small cross.

It's here that the first Christians assembled to honor the tombs of martyrs, pray their prayers in common, and adore the sign of the Redemption.

The horizon is bordered by volcanic rocks. In a clearing, heaven sleeping, still retains the crepuscular tints of evening.

CHORUS OF CHRISTIANS

Alone in the night

Noiselessly,

Let's admire

Let's avoid

With care

All witnesses.

We Christians

Without support.

Yes, let's march

And seek

The Son of God,

The Holy place.

Yes, let's suffer

Affronts

While our eyes

Are on heaven.

The divine port

Is in death.

O Holy Cross

So often

Our hope

Shines this night!

To the meeting

Guide us.

Ray of faith

Yes, arise

In this night,

Nothing shines.

Great God—take pity on us!

We implore you on our knees.

(The Chorus kneels. A ray of light descends from on high to the Cross.)

King of Heaven, master of earth

All Christians adore you on their knees.

You give us the water of salvation,

In faith, Lord, sustain us.

NICANOR

Guards! Disperse this rebel band.

Respect Lilia. Leave me with her!

(To Lilia)

It's you I'm seeking.

LILIA (with a feeling of terror)

Me? What do you want with me?

NICANOR

What are you doing amidst those my wrath pursues?

LILIA

I came on these cold stones,

To pray for the Queen and you.

And for the one who, in our brother's home

Soon must be my spouse.

Weak and in a retired shadow

What can you fear from me?

Ah—let me live unknown

With my love and my faith.

NICANOR

Fear nothing—I love you and I admire

Your beauty, your grace, and your faith.

Each ray of your smile

For me, is a glance from heaven.

My pride bows at your feet.

Your speech troubles my senses.

For angels of the divine voice,

Are only an echo of your accents!

LILIA

Ah, great God—I shiver!

God of chaste loves

Protect me. No one

Is coming to help me!

NICANOR

My palace awaits your presence,

Follow me, come and spend your life there.

Happiness is in power

Happiness dwells in courts.

The Orient, treasure of largesse,

At the sign of my will

Will make all its riches

Adorn your beauty.

LILIA

No—I cannot endure those infamous words.

Helios had my heart and heaven my word.

You, who strengthen the weakness of women

My God, come here! My God, help me.

I will cheat the attempt

Of the traitor who tempts me.

And I mean to remain constant

To my pious love.

For your impious love

Don't imagine that I'll forget

The oath which binds me.

It is written in heaven.

NICANOR

Don't fear the curse of god.

Love baptized me.

I'm Christian since I love you.

I bow before the faith.

Give in to my love that's calling you,

Lilia, don't rebel to such a degree!

The hand of god which made you beautiful

Created your beauty for me.

LILIA

What are you saying? You, Christian! Well, look—

Look around you, Nicanor, say, do you see

What the god of Christians reserves for his real children,

To raise their downtrodden courage?

NICANOR

Your eyes are abused, no, nothing is revealed

In the night I see only a pale limpidity.

It's the uncertain rays of the first star

Which, for my glance alone, lights up your beauty.

LILIA

Ah, you call yourself Christian! And there on this stone

You don't see the light shine on the sign of the elect.

The shadow of Hell has veiled your eyelids.

Trickster! God is protecting me, and I no longer fear you.

NICANOR

Yes, I lied to please you.

My love alone was true

In vain you want to get out of here;

I will follow you everywhere.

My love clasps souls.

You cannot flee your fate—

Because my lips are flames

Which burn until death!

LILIA

God, who sees my danger.

I invoke you fervently

For your unworthy handmaid

Make a miracle, Savior!

Pursued by storm

Open safe harbor for me

Leave honor in my life

Or save me by death.

NICANOR (seizing her)

You shall be mine.

LILIA (struggling)

No!

NICANOR

Mine!

LILIA

No, I tell you.

I will only belong to God.

NICANOR

Your god doesn't hear you.

(Thunder scolds, the earth shakes)

LILIA

God responds with a prodigy

To your blasphemy—

Look!

NICANOR

O Terror! The earth trembles beneath my feet

(overcoming his unease, and with growing fury)

You will be mine.

LILIA

No!

NICANOR

Mine.

LILIA

No, I tell you.

I will belong only to God.

NICANOR

Your God does not exist!

(Hardly have these last words been said, then a new clap of thunderbolts. Nicanor falls, struck by lightning, a moment later, Lilia faints. The stage is plunged into profound darkness. Satan appears.)

SATAN

Here I am free at last. And from the depth of the abyss

I, in God's prison, I can finally emerge.

A century has expired. This was little for the crime

Man has not found a moment to repent.

Now to work! This day is mine.

And let man, crushed beneath the weight of my hate,

Understand from his sorrows that I have broken my chains.

LILIA

Where am I? Ah—My God!

SATAN

Lilia, come to.

From a criminal love your God has preserved you.

But he hasn't saved you from jealousy.

LILIA

O heaven—yes—Nicanor—horrible memory.

I still see his hand prepared to seize me.

Against the divine cross your cursed arm was raised,

O dream—frightful dream!

SATAN

It wasn't a dream!

LILIA

Why, no, it wasn't a dream! Just God!

Helios isn't coming—What's he doing? I shiver.

Is he capable of leaving me alone, at this hour, in this place?

Helios! Helios!

SATAN

Helios is abandoning you!

LILIA

Go! What sinister voice fills my heart with fright?

Helios, abandoning me. No, no get away from me.

It's the voice of Hell! And yet, wretched woman,

How can he leave me in this terrible night?

Who can keep him? Frightful suspicion!

This palace—this queen. Ah, I am losing my mind!

Ah, if I were capable, piercing shadow and space,

Of knowing what's going on in that cursed palace.

SATAN

Your prayers are fulfilled. Look, Lilia!

(The rocks open, and one perceives a dazzling room of riches and light, Helios at the feet of the Queen.)

LILIA

Heaven! What do I see?

Helios at the feet of Olympia!

HELIOS' VOICE (singing)

I want to live forever in the air that you breathe, etc.

LILIA

What profane harmony has soiled my ears?

SATAN

That's your Helios.

LILIA

Are my eyes open?

Is this a nightmare?

SATAN

No, Lilia, you're awake!

LILIA

It's a vision coming to me from Hell!

Helios—wretch! Let's run—Ah, I succumb.

(The vision fades out.)

SATAN

Go! I will put Hell between his heart and you!

(Picking up Nicanor's cape)

I am taking these spoils escaped from the tomb ,

And now I am the Proconsul!

CURTAIN

ACT III
SCENE 3

The Gardens of the Queen. At the back, on a height, the Temple of Hercules Parthenopean. In the nebulous distance Naples as an amphitheater before the gulf of the Bay. In the center, the triumphal column erected by the divine Titus after taking Jerusalem.

CHORUS

O day of intoxication

Day of Happiness

Flee, sadness

Flee, wise behavior

Let's sing in turn

Of Love and Bacchus

Goodbye, wise behavior

Let's sing without cease

Without cease.

HELIOS

This palace, this feast, these flowers, these joy-filled songs.

This celestial beauty. Ah, too cruel image,

Is it really true? Must I believe my eyes?

Or indeed is this the effect of a fancied mirage?

OLYMPIA

No, no—look at me—it's not a lie

Go! You can believe in your happiness

Everything here is real. The rest is only a dream

That you must efface forever from your heart.

It's my love, it's my tenderness

That gives you certain happiness.

No more regrets. Dream of intoxication.

Of the days promised to your destiny.

My hand pulls you

Towards grandeurs.

To you, the Queen

And her splendors.

To you, my soul

My heart is yours.

I am the woman

Who makes you king.

HELIOS

King—I will be king.

(he's seized little by little by his memories, and recalls the rendezvous with Lilia.)

Ah, just heaven—shame, shame on me!

O mortal sorrow—remorse tears me apart!

I had completely forgotten in this fatal delirium

I recall at last—behind me, tempter

Far from my heart

Criminal intoxication.

Lilia, Lilia is calling me.

OLYMPIA

Lilia, Lilia—It's you who hold her fate.

Choose! For you the throne—or death for her!

A BALLET

(During the ballet)

OLYMPIA

Come, o blonde goddess

Smile on our intoxication.

In vain

Time urges us, ceaselessly,

We laugh at its rigors

No frivolous regret

When the hour steals away.

Venus actually consoles us

And makes us victors over time.

CHORUS

Let's love! Venus ravishes hearts

Let's love! No vain regrets!

OLYMPIA

Let's love—free from envy

Let's love—for that is life.

Sad madness

Let one forget it!

Love alone fills our life!

From dusk till dawn

The earth implores it

Let's all love! And love again

To live—that's to love forever!

CHORUS

Let's love—love charms our lives

Let's love—Let's know how to love forever!

CHORUS OF BACCHANTS (male)

Glory to Bacchus

Lyaeus!

Glory to the conqueror of the earth

Glory to the young god! To the god-conqueror

He's king of the earth.

Olympus is his tributary

Let's repeat in chorus:

Glory to Bacchus

It's he who gives us

The autumnal vine

Glory to Bacchus

Lyaeus!

CHORUS of BACCHANTES (females)

Io Bacchus!

Come to this place

O Nysoeus!

O young god!

God of Naxos

Come without delay

Pour waves

Of your nectar.

Io Bacchus!

Rule in this place

Dionysius!

O young god

Let sweet liqueurs

Flow all over the shore

Glory to the strong god

To the conquering god

Io Bacchus!

Yes, of this place.

O Lenoeus

Be the only god.

CHORUS of BACCHANTS (male)

Glory to Bacchus!

Lyoeus!

Glory to the conqueror of the earth

Glory to the young god—to the conqueror god!

He is the king of the earth

Olympus is his tributary.

Glory to Bacchus

He's the one who gives us

Autumnal wine

Glory to Bacchus

Lyoeus.

LILIA

Helios—he's there. It was all true!

HELIOS

Great God!

OLYMPIA

What's this woman coming here for?

LILIA

She's coming to remind the one who forgot her

Of the solemn oath that binds us before God.

Helios—don't you hear? Answer! Answer!

HELIOS

Shut up!

Death is here.

LILIA

Death! I want it! I call it!

HELIOS

Flee, flee, I tell you.

LILIA

Thus—all is over for me.

OLYMPIA

What's this rebel say?

LILIA

I say, Olympia, that for Christian faith

It is sweet to expire under the teeth of lions

Before your faithless court, I confess mine.

And I offer here my life to the God we pray to.

HELIOS

Lilia!

CHORUS

No mercy!

OLYMPIA

Wait! I want to see

Just how far her audacity goes.

LILIA

I believe in God that all heaven reveres.

A God who holds infinity in his hands.

I believe in the blood spilled at Calvary

Where the man-god saved the human race.

In the Holy Spirit, the inspirer of the soul,

Divine torch—passed from shadows

Which levels a dozen tongues of flame

On the cenacle where a dozen Hebrews prayed.

CHORUS

No pardon for her.

Let her go to her fate

The rebel woman

Deserves death.

LILIA

He's the only God who reigns over the world!

One day, the impious will be punished by him.

At his call, all Christians respond.

And may ever his holy name be blessed!

It's He who protects all faithful souls

Near his throne, a glorious throne.

After death life is immortal

And our tomb is the gate of heavens.

CHORUS

No pardon for her

Let her go to her fate.

The rebel woman

Deserves death.

OLYMPIA

Let her be taken away.

HELIOS

Stop!

SATAN (under the features of Nicanor)

Scorn his furor!

LILIA

Him! Him, living. Why no—no, fatal vision.

It's Hell. It's Satan!

SATAN

Eh, what! My noble sister,

The proud Olympia, the beauty without equal,

The idol of the earth, fears a rival.

You want to have her life? Eh, for her—what matters

Death? She has faith—this lie of the heart.

The Christian forever believes heaven's opening its gate

And that with his executioners, death makes him the conqueror.

No, no—for her a more certain punishment. Go—she must live! That will go to your glory!

Let her live! To see until her last moment,

To see Helios on your victory chariot,

To curse her god, to bemoan her lover.

OLYMPIA

Follow her, follow her then if you like!

Run to the desert, poor and joyous

Taste the supreme delights

Of Christian lovers, their vows.

Go, go then, mold from the stone

The hard bread of early ages,

And live on air and prayer,

Under the green dome of palms.

NICANOR

Follow her, follow her then, abandon

Barely sampled pleasures.

Flee the happiness that pride gives.

Pride, that monarch of sensuality.

Flee this Olympia who loves you.

This throne of unparalleled dazzle,

Break this diadem on your face,

That is more radiant than the Sun.

OLYMPIA

Speak, reply, decide.

LILIA

O terrible moments.

SATAN

Speak! Time is rapid!

OLYMPIA

Say a word. I'm waiting for it.

SATAN

See power here.

LILIA

Christian—think of your faith.

OLYMPIA

Finally—break this silence!

HELIOS

O heaven, inspire me!

SATAN

Choose your destiny.

LILIA

Write in the heavens.

OLYMPIA

Horrible or fortunate.

LILIA

Blind—open your eyes.

SATAN

Cease to be rebel.

OLYMPIA

Rebel to my love.

LILIA

My last cry calls you.

HELIOS

Oh—let's flee this court.

OLYMPIA

Still your heart hesitates?

LILIA

Your sister chains herself to you.

SATAN

The Queen once again invites you.

HELIOS

From pity! Leave me alone.

Ah, delirium is here—in my face, in my soul.

What infernal hand has poured this poison there.

What demon's breath burns me with its flame?

It extinguishes my thought and breaks my reason.

LILIA

Helios, I'm calling you

One last time.

When you were faithful to me,

You knew my voice.

Without you, all empires

Would be nothing to me.

This heart which you dismember

Is full only of you.

HELIOS

Lilia. Lilia.

OLYMPIA (to Satan)

Lost for us.

SATAN

Hope.

He's going to abandon her, his precious Lilia.

(To Helios)

Go, then! Go! Dishonor

Her purity

Impure, go live once again

At her side.

For another law

Scorn power.

And with her innocence

Intoxicate yourself.

Go, twice unfaithful

In a single day.

(reaction by Olympia)

Spouse unworthy of her,

Of her love.

Perjured lover

Bear to another mistress

A heart besmirched by intoxication,

A heart that lies.

HELIOS

Truth from Hell! Yes, I've besmirched my soul!

Nothing can absolve me in the eyes of Lilia

Let's save at least her life, if I must live in infamy—!

Queen, I am yours! I love you, Olympia.

(Lilia utters a wrenching scream. She remains for a few moments annihilated by sorrow.)

OLYMPIA

At last you trust my tenderness;

At last love peaks in your heart!

And in my eyes, shining with intoxication

Your glance seeks happiness!

Come, give me all your soul!

Come, you will be the equal of the gods

Yes, my love, divine flame,

My love is going to open the heavens to you.

HELIOS (aside)

Culpable love, cowardly tenderness

I've delivered my heart to you thus.

And the awakening, after intoxication

Comes from my night of double horror—

By saving you, I'm losing my soul.

Lilia—receive my farewells.

Another love, impure flame

Has forever closed the heavens to me.

LILIA

O despair. O frightful day!

The unworthy flame,

Which soils his soul

Has forever closed the heavens to him!

SATAN

He's vanquished! In his soul I have

Revived all the false gods.

With sensuality's dark flame

Go alone to shine at last in his eyes.

Virtue is dead in his soul.

Pleasure alone lives in his heart.

Glory to false gods! Hell take him!

And Satan, Satan is the victor!

CHORUS

Glory to Venus the enchantress.

Glory to the Queen, to the goddess

Whose power troubles his heart.

Glory to Venus the enchantress.

Glory to you, Queen, to you, goddess

Glory to love made victor by you.

CURTAIN

ACT IV
SCENE 4

The Atrium of the palace of Olympia decorated in Etruscan style.

SATAN (alone)

Yes, Satan is victor. The divine wills

Are abandoning this nation to me. It will perish without help.

My power is going to cover this country in ruins.

And eternal night is going to replace their days.

Foolish instrument of destiny which overwhelms it,

Man unites with god to serve my fury.

With unchained slaves an implacable herd

In these shaking walls, terror strolls—

Second me! Come, come, proscribed race,

Victims of pride immolated so many times

Vultures, swoop down over this accursed city

Children of Spartacus, rush to my voice.

(The slaves recoil, seeing the Proconsul.)

What are you afraid of, friends? Know me better.

Eh, what! I am not proscribed like you.

If I've been able to abase myself to flatter a master,

It's to bring him funereal blows.

Now's the time: strike! The gods are with us!

Friends, Let's march!

Let's strike! Let's devastate!

Heaven seconds us,

Friends, let's march!

CHORUS of SLAVES

Let's march!

And may heaven second us.

Let's march

The thunder scolds.

Let's march,

Let's strike.

In the profound night

March

March

Strike

Devastate!

Let's avenge all our affronts

Tremble, masters of the universe

This fertile land

Will pay for our labors

And our wrongs

Rome, the strong

Yes, Rome is dead!

Its reign is quite over!

Its vain wrath

Dies under our blows.

All is ours

The universe is ours

Hear the lightning scold.

From on high, Jupiter seconds us

For Rome, it's the final day.

Let's reign, reign in our turn.

The lightning scolds.

Queen of the world,

It's your last day.

SATAN

Go into the profound night,

Go and break your chains.

And in the world's tears

Avenge all your wrongs suffered!

To you, the good things of life!

To your masters your fate!

The nation is in agony

And tomorrow it will be dead!

The slave is king of the earth,

The slave is master in his turn,

Pride, at last, is going to shut up.

Pride is seeing its last days.

To your masters your fate.

This nation is in agony.

And tomorrow it will be dead.

CHORUS

Let its sleep

Be without awakening.

To us those places,

Loved by the gods.

We will enjoy

We, the living,

It's our turn.

Each has his day.

To us fate.

The slave is stronger.

(In the last part of this scene the noise of thunder increases and mixes with lightning flashes.)

CURTAIN

ACT IV
SCENE 5

The terrace of Olympia's palace.

Aqueducts and temples are visible in the distance.

AT RISE, no sign of the convulsion yet.

HELIOS (enters, agitated)

God has not struck me. The plain is covered

With debris and dead bodies, a nation is expiring,

And the earth beneath me is half open!

What! My crime, o my god—isn't it great enough?

And you, you, Lilia—beneath this celestial wrath

Have you succeeded when God still spares me?

Lilia! Lilia! Vain hope remaining to me

Yes! Heaven has ravished earth of this treasure.

LILIA

I am here!

HELIOS

God be blessed—It's she!

LILIA (with scorn)

Helios blessing heaven!—Withdraw!

HELIOS (entreating)

Lilia!

LILIA

What do you expect? That voice that calls me

Broke my heart and reneged on its word.

HELIOS

My crime deserves eternal torture.

Before God delivers me to it, listen, listen to me!

LILIA

If God disinherits you of eternal happiness

What can you hope for?

HELIOS

I hope in you.

Yes, I've deserved anathema

Which falls on the faces of the accursed

Give me the second baptism;

Return to me all that I've lost!

Let the earth open beneath my feet

For my crime—and in this day

From the bottom of the abyss shall rise

My final cry of love—towards you!

LILIA

What can you hope for of your impure passion?

HELIOS

It's no longer your love that my love demands

Covered with opprobrium, forever unworthy of your prayers,

I implore your pardon—that's all I want.

LILIA

To forgive you!

HELIOS

Tears flood my eyelids.

Ah, don't reject my ardent prayer.

These words are the last exchanged between us.

Time presses! Pity! I implore you on my knees!

LILIA

Ah, despite myself I forget,

His shame and my tears.

At his voice which supplicates,

Effacing my sorrow.

In this profound night

When all is going to finish

On the tomb of the world

Our hands must join.

HELIOS

Angel of heaven! Forget

What the earth has done.

Helios entreats you.

It's your last good deed

In this profound night

When all is going to finish

On the tomb of the world

Our hands must join.

LILIA

My God! This pardon he demands

Like me, deign to give it.

From the high heaven from which grace descends on him

My God—tell me to pardon.

(extending her hands over Helios on his knees before her)

Before God—before whom ascends—in this day of

wrath,

A fervent prayer, from the heart broken by you.

Fulfill my love which you profane.

Since you repent in your last hour,

Helios be pardoned.

HELIOS

Ah, grace from on high touches me!

Predestined ecstasy!

Ah, I feel it, yes, from your mouth—

It's God—God who pardons me.

LILIA

Helios, your impious love affairs

Close the irritated heavens to you.

Though your remorse expiates them.

Come love me in eternity.

Come! Death, which purifies us.

Forever gives you back my love.

Leave this life without regret,

This false happiness which lasts but a day.

Come! Come Follow me, full of hope

Let's go to meet death.

It's eternity which is commencing.

It's love which never ends.

Let's go to heaven, to love again

In heaven where another aurora shines!

Divine place

Of pure love

God makes

Your holy day

Bloom.

HELIOS

Yes, death which punishes us

Forever returns your love to me.

Without regret I leave life,

This false happiness which lasts but a day.

Yes, I'm following you, full of hope

I rush ahead of death

Towards eternity which is commencing.

Towards love that never ends.

Let's go to heaven to love again.

To heaven where another aurora shines.

Divine place

Of pure love

God makes

Your holy day

Bloom.

(Sound of collapsing off stage. The whole chorus rushes in with cries of terror. Meanwhile, the queen in extreme agitation descends the steps of the terrace. Magnus appears behind her)

CHORUS

Night of horror

O Terror

Misfortune!

Misfortune!

Misfortune!

MAGNUS (to Olympians)

Heaven is, in the end, weary of its furors.

Tremble! Here's the moment of supreme terrors

Your reign is complete. That of God begins.

SATAN (offstage)

Olympia!

MAGNUS

Now there's the eternal vengeance

Approaching—look.

SATAN

Olympia.

OLYMPIA

My brother!

Destiny be praised! My brother!

SATAN

Open your eyes!

Your brother succumbed to the blows of thunder;

It's not his voice that calls you.

OLYMPIA

Great Gods!

Who then? Who then are you?

SATAN

I am the God of crime

That you wanted to see this morning.

The king of the dark abyss!

The black archangel.

I am Satan.

OLYMPIA

Satan! O heaven—all abandons me!

All escapes me at once.

SATAN

Yes! You seek in vain

No help, no refuge; an implacable hand

Breaks the last column of your pride.

TOGETHER

OLYMPIA

Moment of agony! O extreme trouble.

Is there then no hope?

Has the supreme moment come?

Is this the end of my power?

SATAN

In your heart full of an extreme trouble

Don't seek a vain hope!

The supreme moment has come

Now's the end of your power.

HELIOS and LILIA

God! Who permits his extreme trouble

Arms our hearts with hope!

Let them see the supreme moment come,

While blessing your holy power!

MAGNUS

Fill their hearts with firm hope,

And until the supreme moment,

Let them bless your holy power.

OLYMPIA

If Olympia must succumb this day

Heaven! Launch your lightning! O earth half open

And excavate for me a royal tomb

In which Herculaneum will be engulfed with me.

(Earth quake, eruption of Vesuvius)

SATAN (pointing out to Olympia the lava that approaches)

There's the punishment.

OLYMPIA

Well—I defy it.

MAGNUS

Christians! Here's death!

HELIOS and LILIA

It's heaven! It's life.

(The palace and the neighboring buildings collapse. Lava descends from the distant crater, and buries under couches of fire this last asylum of queen and people. Finally it clears and all that is left is desolation.

CURTAIN

SARDANAPALUS
BY HENRI BECQUE

CAST OF CHARACTERS

MYRRHA, Greek slave girl

SARDANAPALUS, King of Assyria

BELESES, High Priest

SALEMENE, Brother of the king

ARBACES, Governor of Media

PANIA, Palace Official

A SOLDIER

PRIEST, GRANDEES OF THE EMPIRE, SOLDIERS, WOMAN, comprising the suite of Sardanapalus

ACT I
SCENE 1

Nineveh, Assyria.

The stage represents the precinct reserved for sacrifices. To the right, the entrance to the Temple of Baal.

BELESES:

Behold the day.

The God of Light

Arises and reappears

Without announcing to all Assyria

The terrible decree.

But other gods have spoken in the interim;

I've recognized positive omens

Which are charged with announcing to mortals

The punishment of kings and the end of their race.

ARBACES:

Because of your secret advice, I have left Media

Which only awaits a signal to submit to me.

But over which and over us the king yet commands!

BELESES:

The enterprise is bold;

I've assured myself of friends and soldiers

Won over by my voice against this impious master.

It's you who are going to strike, are you sure of your arm?

ARBACES:

Too powerful to serve under a shadow prince,

I've sworn his death, alone and without your support.

I was hoping he would come to visit my province;

I was expecting that he would make me appear before him.

You came seeking me out and telling me

That the consulted gods were calling me to the empire.

BELESES:

Soon I will make you know

The day that must make all atone,

And from the gown of high priest

Will emerge the arms of a warrior.

ARBACES:

Sovereign power!

Scepter always shining before my eyes!

Ambitious dreams,

Enflame my courage and my hate!

Royal cloak,

Triumphal cloak,

To seize you

I mean to act!

BELESES:

Wait, still

While in this place

My soul implores

The aid of the gods!

I am going to offer to the gods a human victim.

If I read in his blood sure victory

And the success of our plans,

I will place the rest in your hands.

TOGETHER

ARBACES:

One day more to wait,

For the gods to name me king!

BELESES:

The gods are with you.

ARBACES:

I feel that my pride increases,

And that the throne is near me.

BELESES:

You will be king.

(Arbaces leaves.)

BELESES:

I can count on him.

The offer of a crown

Delivers him entirely to me.

He's the one who's going to take it,

And I'm the one who's going to give it.

The high priest will have made a king.

(Enter Salemene)

But who's coming there? Hail Prince Salemene!

What plan brings you hereabouts?

SALEMENE:

I am coming to kneel on your blessed marbles,

To honor with you the gods of my country.

I am coming to take my place at the bloody sacrifice,

That's already been prepared, priest, by your holy hands.

BELESES:

Mighty Baal be once more propitious to us,

Ward off ills and certain crimes!

SALEMENE:

Priest, don't speak of ills and crimes.

If need be, to please the gods, the blood of a victim;

Let's make this blood run in peace,

But only a bold oracle.

Priest, do not arm the wrath

Of the weak against the powerful!

BELESES:

O prince, I can only say

What I've already read

In the precursive signs

Of the most terrible misfortunes!

Noble brother of the king, who respect in him

The crowned heritage of your illustrious race,

Haven't you virtues to guide you and support you?

Why don't you reign in his place?

SALEMENE:

Priest, let's leave on his throne the son

Of great Nimrod and Semiramis.

Let's not raise so high a bold glance.

Perhaps the gods have been irritated against all.

Let's go to their knees

To appease their wrath.

BELESES:

Come then, the victim is ready.

They are bringing him to these parts, laden with chains.

Let's go place ourselves at the head

Of Chaldean priests.

(They enter into the Temple.)

MYRRHA:

(advancing slowly, she is enchained, accompanied by sacrificers)

God of blood, whose image I see,

I am going to be immolated by your savage cult.

Your detested priests dispose of my fate,

But already I was feeling the weight of slavery.

Death will render me free, and I am going to die.

Athens, charming place,

Where my dawn rose,

It's you I still name

At my last moment!

O beloved earth,

Where I was born,

From my first years

Ravishing abode.

What I knew,

What I've lost!

What ill I endure!

I find you again

Before my eyes.

Goodbye forever!

On this earth,

Always beloved,

Light cool breezes

Will no longer be brought to me!

This god of terror and hate

Already hangs his sword over me.

I will never again see the rosy and clear Sun

Lighting the hills of Athens in the morning!

O poetry

Of the Nation,

How distant you are.

I feel my heart full

Of memories

And sighs!

Beautiful mountains,

Beautiful fields,

Roofs of ancestors,

Goodbye, forever!

On this earth,

Always beloved,

Light cool breezes

Will never be brought to me again!

Goodbye forever, my beautiful country!

If I pour tears

Intoxicated with recollections,

Don't fear cowardly alarms,

And I shall know how to die like one of your children,

And yet life was so beautiful!

My morning promised a beautiful evening.

But suddenly, it's death that calls me.

Goodbye, native land, love, pride, hope!

O death, close your somber arms!

Why, formidable goddess,

On the entranceway of youth,

Do you drag me on your path?

But let's show some courage,

Since death breaks the chains

Of slavery.

Death, I love you;

Without extreme sorrow,

I yet see

What I am losing.

Yes, come, o death, break my chains!

(Funereal march. The priests slowly leave the Temple of Baal and come to surround the victim. The High Priest and Salemene enter.)

BELESES:

Baal, terrible and supreme god!

Baal, the greatest of our deities!

Ward off your curse from us,

That you suspend from the heights of the heavens!

We have committed more than one crime,

But see us, at our holy altars,

Offering to you a victim

To spare the criminals!

PRIESTS:

Baal, terrible and supreme god, etc.

MYRRHA:

Ah! I thought death was less hard!

Hour of terror, of torture!

O terrible moment! Odious sacrifice

That demands blood to honor the gods!

Strength abandons me.

I fear, I tremble, and I shiver;

Around me I have no one

To receive my farewells.

BELESES, PRIESTS:

Baal, terrible and supreme god, etc.

(The refrain of the funeral march is interrupted by the arrival of Sardanapalus. The king enters preceded by young dancers and players of instruments.)

SARDANAPALUS:

Stop! Where are you leading her?

BELESES:

To god who demands her!

SARDANAPALUS:

High Priest, I am weary of so many cruelties.

Do you think what pleases your divinities

Is the death of a child, of a woman?

BELESES:

Do you know better than I,

Would you teach me the law,

That I've studied since childhood?

My piety, my lore

Are greater than yours.

SARDANAPALUS:

Nothing is greater than your king.

BELESES:

Guilty king, may nothing touch you.

Baal has brought you here.

You are going to hear from my mouth

The oracle of the god of gods.

As for me, who reads in the stars,

And who knows the secret of the ethers,

I predicted disasters

That the lightning predicted to me.

The winds roll with threats

And in the vast emptiness

Shine cursed icons;

I see Baal descending,

I see your crown in ashes,

And your palace destroyed.

Misfortune on this country!

SARDANAPALUS:

(going to Myrrha) Being divine, slight form

Made to charm and seduce,

How sweet and dear your beauty is to me.

I am the master of the earth

Coming to save you!

BELESES:

Child, you belong to me! Pure and noble victim.

It is a different torture, alas much more cruel!

The misfortune is worth more than the crime.

Choose the harem or the altar!

SARDANAPALUS:

Being divine, slight form

Made to charm and seduce.

How sweet and dear your beauty is to me!

TOGETHER

SARDANAPALUS:

I am the master of the earth

Coming to save you.

BELESES:

The misfortune is worse than the crime.

Flee the harem, climb to the altar!

MYRRHA:

Resign yourself, poor victim,

To this cruel torture;

Flee the harem, climb to the altar!

MYRRHA:

Priest, I want to die.

SARDANAPALUS:

And the king forbids it.

Pania, break the chains which hold this child

And lead her immediately to my palace.

Priest do you think your hate

Capable of arresting my path?

Your victim is mine! How your wrath bursts out!

Come then to take her in my arms

To the party I am giving tonight on the Euphrates!

Love calls us to the palace.

Friends, imitate your king;

Feast a new slave girl

That you must adore as I do!

TOGETHER

BELESES:

Impious and cowardly king!

SALEMENE, PANIA:

Imprudence of the king!

MYRRHA:

I am the slave of their king.

SARDANAPALUS, CHORUS:

Love calls us to the palace, etc.

CURTAIN

ACT II
SCENE 2

The stage represents the gardens of the palace. At the right, a pavilion and marble gallery. In the distance, the Euphrates flows.

Party. Sardanapalus, stretched on a bed in the form of a throne, dominates the guests, grouped on couches around him here and there.

Myrrha is standing near the king. Night is coming on.

CHORUS:

Let us again, let us leave the hours

To flow without uproar;

May the feast never cease and die,

Except with the night.

Sweet abandon! Cherished laziness!

Brilliant palace! Passionate climate!

Beloved men, remain without cease

To sigh in our arms!

Let us again, let us leave the hours

To flow without uproar;

May the feast never cease and die,

Except with the night.

King, king of the earth,

Your people, each day,

Under your tutelary hand,

Is changing its cries of war

Into a long love song.

The new maxims,

Which fall from your hands,

Make women more beautiful

And men more humane.

King, king of the earth,

Your people, each day,

Under your tutelary hand,

Is changing its cries of war

Into a long love song.

(The guests are kneeling.)

SARDANAPALUS:

Rise, Myrrha!

The whole world adores me,

And renders homage to my blessings,

But I form other desires.

I still need your love.

MYRRHA:

They adore you!

But in the noble land,

That saw my birth,

They didn't teach me

To bend at the feet of a master.

SARDANAPALUS:

Well, in your noble country,

They boast divine poets.

Sing, Myrrha, the marriages they made;

Sing, Myrrha, for a submissive lover.

MYRRHA:

Muse of my country,

With a bronze lyre,

Come closer, they invite you

To this royal feast,

You who sing the history

Of a nation free and strong,

They offer you to drink

In a cup of gold.

The haughty and pure muse

Is not seated in your home?

The eagle doesn't fly in a dark cloud,

The virgin doesn't want an old man for a spouse.

Muse of my land,

In our cradles you place

Scorn of life

And love of heroes.

O sisters of my youth,

Live your entire days

On the earth of Greece,

In the arms of your warriors.

To their valiant souls,

Attach yourselves forever

They can show you brilliant wounds;

They can tell you of Glory as well as love.

SARDANAPALUS:

Always man is prodigal with blood,

Always with battles and death;

I prefer to live without effort;

I prefer to die without remorse.

Let's drink! Our tables are filled

With exquisite meats and divine fruits;

The juice of perfumed liqueurs

Makes us believe in distant worlds.

And we have only a few years

Which are slipping through our hands.

Drink up. Let them dispose

Of such a short respite

To celebrate the corn,

The grape and the rose!

Let's love! Beloved slaves,

Leaving the intoxication of feasts

In the shadow of decorated couches.

Let's prolong our sweet morns,

And we have only a few years

Which are slipping through our hands.

Let's love! Let them dispose, etc.

CHORUS:

Let's love! Let them dispose, etc.

SALEMENE:

(entering) Lord!

SARDANAPALUS:

What do you want with me?

Your presence is new at banquets with your king.

SALEMENE:

Lord, danger alone brings me.

For today, leave this cup as yet full,

For once be prudent.

SARDANAPALUS:

Time enough tomorrow! Tomorrow for business!

SALEMENE:

Already the hour has struck!

Already the time is his!

Tomorrow you will resume your customary dreams,

But let's wake up today.

SARDANAPALUS:

(who has removed his crown of roses)

Light crown,

That I love and prefer

To crowns of gold,

I must toss you away, my dear,

And you aren't faded yet.

(The guests withdraw; Myrrha is disposed to follow them, she is retained by the king.)

SARDANAPALUS:

Myrrha! My Greek girl withdraws,

My Greek girl flees, when I become king again.

MYRRHA:

Watch your health and your empire.

SALEMENE:

Lord, hear me.

SARDANAPALUS:

Child, withdraw.

(Myrrha distances herself.)

SARDANAPALUS:

Myrrha! Return, let me give you

A single kiss as sweet as your voice.

MYRRHA:

Protect your head and your crown.

SALEMENE:

Lord, hear me.

SARDANAPALUS:

Child, withdraw.

(Myrrha leaves.)

SALEMENE:

Do you intend to hear me and not dream?

I am coming in time to save you.

SARDANAPALUS:

Speak! Speak! The night is pure.

Under the heavens,

Already all rests and murmurs

On the heaving breast of nature,

Exhaling an amorous sigh.

Speak! Speak! Say what you want,

SALEMENE:

When hate and daring

Already arm your enemies

To destroy in a single day your empire and your race,

Do you still recline in these sleepy parts?

Are you waiting to show your courage

When their sword is striking you?

SARDANAPALUS::

Go, I have lived like a wise man

And I will know how to die like a king.

SALEMENE:

Media is on fire. An important dispatch

Announces to me the conspiracies and the departure of Arbaces.

SARDANAPALUS:

Arbaces! Is it really he who threatens me?

I left him his title and his governorship

For the fidelity he showed to my father.

SALEMENE:

The scepter was then in the hand of a warrior,

And the ambitious choose their time.

In this palace of infamous joys,

Cursed palace,

They obey you;

Around the bed where you sleep,

Your toadies,

On your face crowned with roses,

Burn incense.

But this Arbaces, who braves you

And who conspires in peace,

Will hunt you like a slave

From your palace.

Your ancestors, whom the people admire,

Proud and haughty,

Used to scour their empire

As sovereigns.

They made their crown shine,

Their sword, too.

And you conceal your person

Always here.

But Arbaces, who braves you

And conspires in peace,

Will hunt you like a slave

From your palace.

SARDANAPALUS:

You say my people are rising?

SALEMENE:

A revolt led by malcontents.

SARDANAPALUS:

But if my hand grasps the sword,

Their repentance will be bloody.

(pause)

Look at this peaceful night.

My people are sleeping in peace.

Far from me, useless terror,

Love, god of the night, watch over my palace.

SALEMENE:

Go, you are no longer king of Assyria;

You are no longer king, you are no longer king.

SARDANAPALUS:

Well, protect my folly.

It's you who are going to reign for me.

(going to the back)

Take the crown and the royal purple;

Take the scepter of gold, the sword of battles.

To you, divine honors and triumphal parades,

Command the council, the vassals, the soldiers.

(The Chorus enters, slaves bear the royal insignia. Sardanapalus and the slaves place the royal mantle on Salemene.)

SARDANAPALUS:

Cover yourself with the cloak

That my hand abandons to you.

Obey. I order it.

The burden of power, the defense of the throne,

All rest on you.

Honor, honor to the king.

CHORUS:

Honor, honor to the king!

ARBACES:

(appearing in the pavilion and pointing to Salemene)

One step raises me to the throne or hurls me in the abyss!

Terrible visions which precede crime,

Don't make my arm or my dagger tremble.

Let him die!— It is too late.

(Sardanapalus retires. The guests have resumed the places they occupied at the beginning of the scene. Salemene casts off his cape.)

SALEMENE:

Get up and let's fight.

Abandon your party beds.

CHORUS:

Let's drink! Let's drink!

SALEMENE:

Leave off love and singing

When the sword is over your head.

CHORUS:

Let's love! Let's love!

SALEMENE:

They don't hear me;

They are deaf to the voice which speaks of battles.

O my country, o city of my fathers,

Which hurls so much luster on earth

Between your sisters you shone most

In the heavens your star is going to pale.

I hear the storm

And my courage

Cannot save you from shipwreck.

The winds are driving you to shore.

Yes, I see you destroying yourself on the waves,

And sure of your end, I shed my tears.

Empire of Assyria,

I am making a useless effort to save you.

Let me find death

Rather than be present at your fall, O Fatherland!

CHORUS:

(falling asleep) Allow us still, allow us a few hours

To spend without disturbance;

Let the feast not cease and die

Except with the night.

SALEMENE:

O Fatherland

Hear them!

Impious feast!

The noise of the battles they are forgetting

Will come to awaken this palace.

(He falls annihilated on the couch previously occupied

by Sardanapalus. Night has come. Arbaces reappears and advances prudently through the sleeping groups. Ritornelle. The king crosses the back of the stage dragging Myrrha. Arbaces stops, and when they've passed runs to Salemene and kills him. At the scream uttered by Salemene, the Chorus awakes.)

CHORUS:

A scream of agony and distress

Comes to surprise us in our intoxication.

The prince! O cruel spectacle.

He's been struck a mortal blow.

SARDANAPALUS:

What is this uproar that comes to trouble my peace?

PANIA:

It's a scream of sorrow, it's a signal of war.

A traitor, an assassin has entered the palace.

SARDANAPALUS:

What's he say?

PANIA:

Look.

SARDANAPALUS:

Ah! My brother, my brother!

Last support of the throne, proud and heroic soul!

The blow which struck you must strike the king.

I am going to avenge your death or die with you.

Soldiers, soldiers awake.

Under the standard of my fathers,

Of your ancient wars

Have memory, friends.

Let's march! Our bold steps

Will surprise these daredevils.

Of your ancient wars

Have memory, friends.

Arm your arms

For battle;

Spill the blood of these rebels.

Faithful soldiers,

Lead me;

Show your king the way!

(They bring a sword and cuirass to Sardanapalus.)

MYRRHA:

What new feeling grips my spirit!

Great king! You are no more a barbarian!

You are rising like a hero from the bed of sensuality.

Ah! Stay this way! I think I'm seeing Achilles himself.

Dragging his untamed brothers to battle.

I love you!

SARDANAPALUS:

(then the Chorus)

Soldiers, soldiers awake, etc.

CURTAIN

ACT III
SCENE 3

A dusty road near Nineveh.

BELESES:

Our astonished soldiers have fled like women

At the very aspect of the king standing in their path.

They are already pursuing with their infamous outcries

The priest who put arms in their hands.

Baal, cast a favorable glance

On your faithful servant;

Protect your humble adorer.

Face in the dust,

I was living in prayer,

Despairing guardian

Of your sacred temple.

Weeping in the shadow,

This somber and detested

Reign,

Demanding mercy

For so much audacity

And impiety.

One day I thought I heard you and your powerful voice

Exhorting me to punish and overthrow the king.

I took up the sword for your glory,

Priest and soldier of your altars,

You hold victory in your hand,

You've given it to criminals.

I see your name and your memory

In man's home fallen into scorn

And your temples will be destroyed.

CHORUS:

(of Priests and soldiers, entering)

Misfortune on you.

Priest without faith,

Who promised miracles.

Misfortune on you.

Priest without faith,

You lied to us in your oracles.

BELESES:

Men without piety, conspirators without virtue,

Allow the gods time to accomplish their miracles.

Wait, and don't flee any more.

ARBACES:

Cursed priest, you promised me the empire.

The gods, you told me, will battle with us.

This great king seemed to you so easy to destroy

When you saw the people groveling at his feet.

REFRAIN BY CHORUS:

Misfortune on you, etc.

BELESES:

(cupping his ear) What's that uproar?

(enter a soldier)

Soldier, what news?

SOLDIER:

The Euphrates is overflowing.

BELESES:

The Euphrates has overflowed!

This miracle, soldiers, that your voice calls for,

The god who leads us has just granted us.

ARBACES:

The Euphrates has overflowed! Repeat your message.

SOLDIER:

The stream, swelled, already on its passage

Has filled the ditches and destroyed the ramparts

Which in an instant, are going to collapse.

The people loudly curse Sardanapalus.

We can attack the royal dwelling

Whose trembling soldiers will die under our daggers.

BELESES:

Soldiers, see down there the river overflowing.

Be grateful for the support the gods are giving you.

This dazzling miracle, that their hand grants to you,

Must give courage to pious men.

To Baal address your ardent prayers.

He will pardon your doubts, your terrors.

He will make you conquerors.

ARBACES AND THE CHORUS:

Inspired priest, lead us to battle;

We will march at your heels.

CURTAIN

ACT III
SCENE 4

A Hall in the Palace.

MYRRHA:

Silence and night spread their alarms;

Two long days have passed without news of the king.

Ah! If he dies, I will die! The distant flash of arms

Shines at intervals and freezes me with terror.

O king, if fate abandons you,

My life is yours forever.

They can take your crown from you

But love's crown you will keep.

The scepter is a burden

That overwhelms and crushes you;

Let it go to live near me

For our hearts

Let's seek at the foot of the Caucasus

A valley embedded with flowers.

Strangers to the uproars of the earth,

There we will live in the mystery.

The charming echo of this retreat

Will only hear words of love.

Ah! Come, let's carry to a solitary place

Our two hearts irrevocably united

O king, if fate abandons you, etc.

But the uproar of combats is getting closer— Great gods!

I see our enemies everywhere victorious.

The king is fighting in this crowd

He is wounded— I've seen his blood being shed.

SARDANAPALUS: (entering)

The battle is lost.

I am going to rejoin my ancestors.

PANIA:

Flee, lord, reach an unknown plain

From which you will reassemble more numerous help.

SARDANAPALUS:

What are you speaking of flight for?

No! I will not flee!

Triumphant traitors are advancing on our heels,

They would like, slaves in fury,

To take Sardanapalus alive.

I order you instantly to set the palace ablaze!

Those who have loved me will remain; for the others,

Those who have never had hearts like ours,

I allow them to go in peace to surrender to the conquerors.

PANIA:

What are you requiring of me? Death and conflagration.

SARDANAPALUS:

I wish it.

PANIA:

Reject this impious thought.

SARDANAPALUS:

I order you immediately to set this palace ablaze!

(Exit Pania.)

SARDANAPALUS:

(to Myrrha) Didn't you hear the order I've given?

Leave instantly; depart.

MYRRHA:

I'm staying.

SARDANAPALUS:

What's she saying?

She hesitates to flee this funereal place.

Our hour has struck.

After having saved you once from death,

Do you think that my hand condemns and drives you to it?

MYRRHA:

Here death is sweet,

I will die in your arms.

SARDANAPALUS:

No! No! You won't die!

Noble woman,

Love fills your soul,

But I must

Perish without you.

Your youth is there calling you.

To die so soon, why that's dying twice.

MYRRHA:

No, I am dying without regrets.

I mean to leave with you, in flames,

So that even death will forever

Unite our souls!

SARDANAPALUS:

The fire's lit, time presses,

Yet one more caress,

And then think to flee;

I alone wish to die.

MYRRHA:

The fire's lit, time presses,

Yet one more caress,

And let's seek in death

An eternal ecstasy.

SARDANAPALUS:

Let me order you to live.

MYRRHA:

In your arms danger intoxicates me.

Let's demand of death

An eternal ecstasy.

SARDANAPALUS:

Goodbye, sweet and faithful friend,

A single kiss, and then think of your life.

MYRRHA:

No, I am dying without regrets.

I mean to leave with you, in flames,

So that even death will forever

Unite our souls!

TOGETHER

SARDANAPALUS:

Ah! Your youth and your life,

Your heart sacrifices them to me.

But hear my voice, which screams to you,

Myrrha, flee death!

MYRRHA:

Ah! My youth and my life,

My heart sacrifices to you.

Hear my voice, which screams to you,

I mean to share your fate.

SARDANAPALUS:

Get out of here! The sword approaches and the palace is set ablaze. You've only got a moment.

MYRRHA:

And you, you would die alone,

Without friends and without wife.

This funeral pyre belongs to me,

As I to you, my lover.

SARDANAPALUS:

Get out of here.

MYRRHA:

I'm staying.

SARDANAPALUS:

Well, you wish it;

Let's die together!

TOGETHER:

The fire's lit, time presses,

Yet one more caress.

Let's demand of death

An eternal ecstasy.

CURTAIN

ACT III
SCENE 5

The funeral pyre.

SARDANAPALUS, MYRRHA, THE CHORUS:

Let's love until the last hour!

Let's love in the arms of death!

We are departing for another dwelling

Where we can love again!

(Conflagration.)

CURTAIN

ABOUT THE EDITOR

Frank J. Morlock has written and translated many plays since retiring from the legal profession in 1992. His translations have also appeared on Project Gutenberg, the Alexandre Dumas Père web page, Literature in the Age of Napoléon, Infinite Artistries.com, and Munsey's (formerly Blackmask). In 2006 he received an award from the North American Jules Verne Society for his translations of Verne's plays. He lives and works in México.

www.ingramcontent.com/pod-product-compliance
Lightning Source LLC
LaVergne TN
LVHW041626070426
835507LV00008B/468